Kids'
Guide

Governments
Around the World

Ernestine Giesecke

Heinemann Library

Customer Service 888-454-2279
Visit our website at www.heinemannlibrary.com

Designed by Jennifer Carney
Printed in Hong Kong

04 03 02 01
10 9 8 7 6 5 4 3 2

Library of Congress Cataloging-In-Publication Data
Giesecke, Ernestine, 1945-
    Governments around the world / Ernestine Giesecke.
        p. cm. – (Kids' guide)
    Includes bibliographical references and index.
    Summary: Introduces the concept of government, exploring various types of systems,
including democracy, communism, and socialism, and presenting international
organizations such as the UN and NATO.
    ISBN 1-57572-511-8 (library binding)
    1. Comparative government—Juvenile literature. [1. Comparative government.] I. Title.
II. Series.
JF127.G54 2000
320.3—dc21
                                                        99-057610

Acknowledgments
The publishers would like to thank the following for permission to reproduce photographs:
Bettmann/Corbis, p. 4; AP/Wide World, pp. 5, 6, 11, 12, 13, 14, 18, 19, 24, 27; Hugo Fast, p. 7;
Marleen Daniels/Impact Visual, p. 15; Tomas Mira/Sodergren/Impact Visual, p. 16; Corbis, p.
17; Blaine Harrington III, p. 20; Jean-Jacques Grezet/Sygma, p. 21; Canadian Press Picture
Archive, p. 22; David R. Austen/Uniphoto, p. 23; Sean Sprague/Impact Visual, p. 25;
Reuters/Corbis, p. 26; Robert Kalina/Impact Visuals, p. 28; Raymond Reuter/Sygma.

Cover: AP/Wide World

The publisher would like to thank Susan Temple, of the North Carolina Department of Public
Instruction, and Jay Adler for their comments in the preparation of this book.

Every effort has been made to contact copyright holders of any material reproduced in this book.
Any omissions will be rectified in subsequent printings if notice is given to the publisher.

Note to the reader: Some words are shown in bold, **like this.**
You can find out what they mean by looking in the glossary.

Contents

What Is Government?

A government is the organization of people that directs the actions of a nation, state, or community. A government has the **authority** and power to make, carry out, and **enforce** laws, and to settle disagreements about those laws.

Governments have many different structures. Some governments have similar structures, but they act very differently.

The people who lead governments come to power in different ways. Some government leaders are elected, or chosen by the citizens. Other governments are led by people who are related to a previous ruler. Still others are led by people who force their way into power.

Governments may have limited or unlimited power. Power is most often limited by a written **constitution.** In countries with constitutions, both the people and the government know and follow accepted rules.

When a group of people have their own government and live within a defined territory, they are known as a nation. There are more than 200 nations in the world today.

When a government has limited power, people can speak out to let the government know what they want.

St. Peter's square is part of Vatican City, Italy.

In some countries without a constitution, individuals have given themselves unlimited powers. These governments have power over every aspect of people's lives. These governments expect the people to follow strict rules while the government itself follows no rules.

The United States is one of several countries that have a **federal** system. In federalism, governmental power is shared between a central government and divisions of the country, such as states or **provinces.** Canada, Argentina, and Australia are some other federalist countries.

Vatican City is a separate nation—the world's smallest—located within the city of Rome, Italy. It is the home of the Pope, the leader of the Roman Catholic Church.

Most nations have a single central government. Countries with a **monarch,** such as Sweden and Japan, have single governments. France and the Philippines are one-government countries without a monarch.

The Jobs of Government

All governments have some of the same jobs. The most important job is protection. A government must protect itself as well as the people it leads. It should be strong enough to defend against threats from both inside and outside the country.

Many governments also want to protect the rights of individuals. Such governments make laws to prevent people and organizations—even the government itself—from interfering with a person's rights. In some countries, however, the government itself harms people, such as by putting them in prison without a trial.

The army in Israel is always alert, ready to protect the nation and its government from outside attack.

One of the jobs of a government is to do things that will bring honor to the nation. The race to put a man on the moon gave the entire United States a goal and helped citizens feel pride in their government.

A government should have a clear and fair way to settle differences among the people it governs. One way most governments do this is through the use of laws and courts.

Another job of a government is to manage the country's resources. These are money, the **raw materials** needed to make products, and the people needed to make those products. The government's job is to make sure that people can earn enough money to buy the things they need. This is difficult to do in some countries—either because the resources are scarce or because the government keeps tight control of the resources.

Governments of the World

These are some of the countries you will read about in this book.

Canada

United States

New York
Washington, D.C.

Mexico

Cuba

Brazil

Republic

Constitutional monarchy

Monarchy

Dictatorship/military government

Communist

Confederation

Other

Constitutional Governments

A **constitution** is a **document** that describes the **authority** and power of a government. It tells what powers the government has and describes the limits of those powers.

A constitution usually describes how power is passed from one person to another. It tells when and how people can be elected, as well as who is qualified to be elected. It also might tell how long a person can remain in power.

Many nations with written constitutions are **democracies** or **republics.** In such nations, the people elect, or choose, their leaders. The United States is a democracy. Here, the authority and power for making, **enforcing,** and explaining laws is shared among three branches of government. There is a **chief executive,** a **legislature,** and a top, or supreme, court. Each has a special job to do. No one person or branch can get too much power.

A constitution
• describes the government
• lists the purposes of the government
• describes the rights of the people
• defines and limits the powers of the leaders
• tells how leaders are elected and how long they can stay in office

The United States Constitution, approved by nine states in 1787, is the world's oldest written constitution.

Like presidents in other countries with constitutional governments, the French president reports to the legislature on the country's well-being.

Some countries have constitutions that are written by or changed by a few powerful people. These constitutions are more like statements telling who is in charge, and they do not describe any limits to the government's power. This may result in unlimited, **authoritarian,** or even **totalitarian** governments.

The United States of America is a **federal** republic. The head of government, the president, is elected by the people. Members of the legislature also are elected by the people.

France is a republic. Its president, the **chief of state,** is elected. The head of government is the prime minister, appointed by the president. Members of the legislature (the National Assembly) are elected. France has a **free-market economy,** but the government owns railway, electricity, aircraft, and telephone companies.

Monarchies

A monarchy is a government led by a single permanent ruler, usually a king or a queen. This ruler, called a **monarch,** often gains power from his or her parents or another relative.

There are not many true monarchies left in the world today. However, monarchs rule several countries in North Africa and the Middle East, often with the king as an **absolute ruler.** This may result in an **authoritarian**—or even **totalitarian**—government.

The United Kingdom (sometimes called Britain) is a constitutional monarchy, but its government is more like a democracy. It has both a monarch and a **constitution.** The constitution is not completely written as a single document. Instead, it consists of many laws passed over the centuries. The **legislature** has two houses: the House of Lords and the House of Commons. There is a prime minister, who is the head of the government. The leader of the **political party** with the most seats in the house of commons becomes the prime minister.

*In a constitutional monarchy, the duties of the monarch are mostly ceremonial. Here, Queen Elizabeth of Great Britain speaks to the **parliament.***

This procession honors His Majesty King Bhumibol Adulyadej, who has served as Thailand's monarch for over 50 years.

Some countries have both a monarch and a constitution. In these countries, the king or queen acts as the head of state. He or she represents the country to the rest of the world. The monarch of a constitutional monarchy plays an important role in national events but usually does not have great **political** power. The country is actually ruled by people who are elected according to the constitution.

There are few absolute monarchies left on earth. Saudi Arabia was an absolute monarchy until 1992. Since then, the king has been elected, but only by members of his royal family.

Dictatorships

Sometimes the government of a country just doesn't work well. Perhaps most of the people are poor and hungry, and people working in government use their positions to take money for doing favors. These things make the government weak.

When a government is weak, other people may try to take it over. Often, members of the **military overthrow** the government. This is because military forces have power and weapons.

Libya is a military dictatorship. Muammar al-Qaddafi overthrew a monarchy in 1969 and took over as **chief of state.** He rewrote the **constitution** and established a **legislature** called the General People's Congress. It is run by a single **political party**, his own.

Muammar al-Qaddafi, right, meets with Yasir Arafat, the leader of the Palestinian Liberation Organization.

In Iraq, Saddam Hussein demands respect and loyalty from all citizens.

Once the military has taken over the government, the new leaders may begin to make changes. They might decide that the constitution, if one existed, should be put aside for a while. The military leader becomes a dictator—an **absolute ruler.** He or she may establish his or her own rules and ignore the laws of the country.

A dictatorship is often a **totalitarian** government. Because dictators do not want the people to know the truth about what is happening, they usually take control of the newspapers and television stations. They also may prevent people from gathering in groups in order to keep them from fighting the new government. Dictators usually severely punish people who publicly disagree with them.

On paper, the government of Iraq is a **republic.** However, Saddam Hussein, in power since 1979, acts like a dictator. He is both chief of state and head of government. There is one political party, led by Saddam Hussein—no other parties are allowed. The president and his friends have nearly total control of manufacturing and trade.

Socialism

A government can also be described by the way it manages a nation's **economic** resources. A country's resources include natural resources, such as iron ore to make steel and good soil to grow food. It also includes human resources, such as workers who mine the iron ore, turn it into steel, and then form it into tractors, or farmers who plant crops, harvest them, and bring them to market.

Socialism is one way governments can manage a country's resources. One of the goals of a **socialist** government is to give all citizens an equal share in the products and services of the country. Generally, a socialist government tries to achieve this equality by creating and then following an economic plan that affects all parts of society.

Sweden's economy is a combination of **free-market** and socialism. Most of the country's economy is privately owned, but the country has a **welfare** system that gives all citizens **benefits,** such as health care and retirement income.

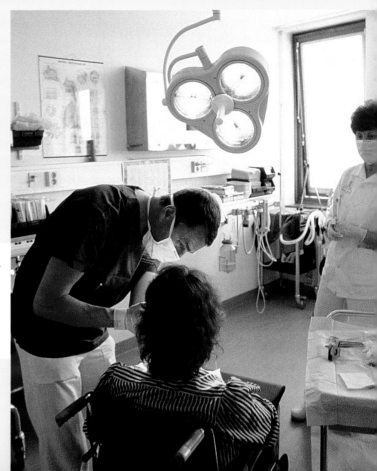

Income taxes in Sweden are among the highest in the world because the government provides free health care and child care to its citizens.

The government of Norway owns and runs nearly all of the railroads in the country.

In many socialist countries, the government controls all large businesses that affect everyone, such as railroads, airlines, and telephones. In some cases, the government itself owns and manages the businesses. In other cases, the businesses are owned by individuals but are under the government's tight control.

Norway is a constitutional monarchy with a king as **chief of state.** The head of government, the **prime minister,** is appointed by the king and approved by the **legislature.**

A socialist government requires people who work to give a large part of what they make to the government, usually as income tax. The government uses this money to provide benefits for all the people. This way, even citizens who can't work can still have a good life. Many socialist governments offer all citizens free health care, free education, affordable housing, and a comfortable retirement income.

17

Communism

Communism is another way a government can manage the country's resources. Under this system of government, the people own all the resources, including farms, factories, and stores.

In a **communist** country, the leaders of the Communist Party make important government decisions. They decide the **economic** plan and how it will be carried out. There may be an elected **legislature,** but it usually has little power. Programs proposed by the Communist Party leaders are automatically approved.

Cuba is a communist nation. The government controls all farming, industry, and foreign trade. The **chief of state** and head of government is Fidel Castro Ruz, whose army captured power in 1959. There is an elected legislature, but there is only one **political party.**

When students in the People's Republic of China spoke out against government policy, the government sent the army to silence them.

*From 1917 until 1991, the communist government of the **Soviet Union** controlled every aspect of production in the country.*

The government plans what resources will be used and who will use them. It also plans what products will be made and who will make them. Finally, the government decides how the finished products, as well as the **profits** from them, will be divided among the people.

People in communist countries are often told what kind of work they can do. They are told whether they can become a college professor or a factory worker. Both college professors and factory workers are paid by the government, and may earn about the same amount.

Countries with a communist economic system usually have an **authoritarian** or **totalitarian** government. Only the communist political party is recognized, and disagreement with the government is not allowed.

Free Markets

Some governments choose not to be involved in the production of goods or in the creation of services. Instead, they help privately owned businesses grow and prosper. This situation is called a **free-market economy,** or **capitalism.**

Singapore has a free-market economy. The country and its people profit from their work. Singapore is a **republic** within a group of countries called a commonwealth. The president is the **chief of state** and is elected by **popular vote.** Members of the **legislature** also are elected by popular vote. However, there is only one major **political party,** which makes the government somewhat **authoritarian.**

Singapore does not have many natural resources, but it has a large labor force. Singapore specializes in manufacturing items that require a lot of labor.

In a free-market economy, an individual, like this craftsman, is able to make and sell as many, or as few, items as he or she wishes.

In nations with free markets, the people and the government work together to make a **profit.** People who supply **raw materials,** those who make products, and those who sell the products work together. In a free-market economy, the government often allows individuals and companies to sell their products and services for as much as other people or companies are willing to pay.

Japan has a free-market economy. It is also a constitutional monarchy. There are two legislative houses, whose members are elected. There are many political parties.

Empires and Commonwealths

There are no true empires in the world today. An empire was a group of different countries held together by military force. The people in the countries in an empire had different ways of living, different backgrounds, and different languages, but they were ruled by the strongest country in the group.

Britain once had one of the largest empires in the world. For three hundred years, from the mid-1600s to the mid-1900s, the British Empire included places as far apart as Canada and Australia and as different as Hong Kong and South Africa. Britain created the empire primarily to get the **raw materials** to make new products and to create new places to sell those products.

Canada is a member of the Commonwealth of Nations. Canada's government is a **democracy.** Its **chief of state** is the British monarch, who is represented in Canada by a governor. Queen Elizabeth II of Britain chooses the governor with the advice of Canada's **prime minister,** who is the head of the country's government and the leader of the major **political party.** Canada has a **free-market** economy.

Government leaders of Canada talk with their Prime Minister, Jean Chretien, third from the left in the front row.

A commonwealth is a group of countries that forms for the good (the "common wealth") of all its member countries. The largest commonwealth is the Commonwealth of Nations, formed of more than 50 nations that were once part of the British Empire. The leaders of Commonwealth nations meet to discuss matters of importance to all the countries and to work toward common **economic** goals.

The Commonwealth of Independent States is made up of twelve nations that were formerly part of the **Soviet Union.** This commonwealth was formed to help keep the peace between countries that had been under tight **communist** rule.

The Great Barrier Reef of Australia was once part of the British Empire. Today, Australia and other countries are part of the Commonwealth of Nations.

The United Nations

At different times in history, countries have chosen to work together. Sometimes, several nations joined forces against a country that had more wealth or power.

After **World War II,** some nations decided to work together in order to avoid war in the future. These nations formed the United Nations, or UN. The United Nations is not a government. It does not make laws and has no army. Instead, the United Nations provides a way for governments to work out their differences.

Everything that is said during a meeting of the UN is translated into many languages, so that everyone will understand.

The UN Charter lists four purposes: "to maintain international peace and security, to develop friendly relations among nations, to cooperate in solving international problems and in promoting respect for human rights, and to be a center for harmonizing the actions of nations."

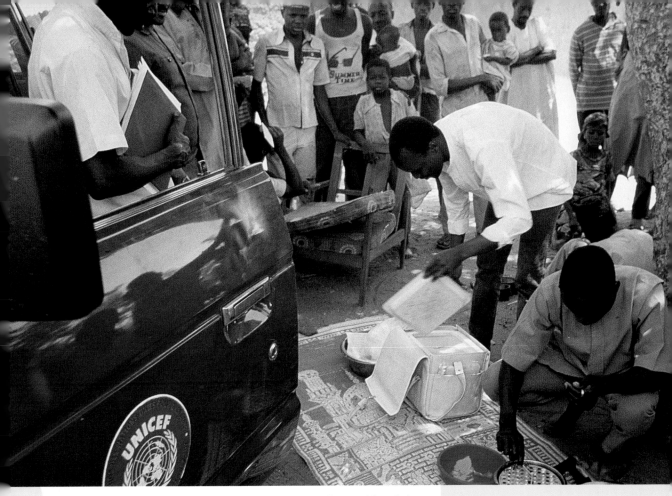

The UN has sent medical workers throughout the world to help countries control or wipe out deadly diseases.

The countries that started the United Nations in 1945 wrote a statement, called the UN Charter, describing their plans. Member countries promise to live together in peace and to work together to keep the rest of the world peaceful without having to use force. They voluntarily supply peacekeeping forces made up of soldiers who can be sent to areas where local **conflict** threatens peace.

Countries that belong to the United Nations also work together to improve the health and living conditions of people around the world. They help people recover and rebuild from disasters such as floods and earthquakes.

The United Nations was founded in 1945 by 51 nations, including the United States. Today, 185 nations belong. The main offices of the United Nations are in New York City. There are other UN offices in Geneva, Switzerland; Nairobi, Kenya; and Vienna, Austria.

Other International Organizations

In today's world, there are many different groups of nations that work together for various purposes. Some are alliances, which are groups of countries pledged to support one another in times of **conflict.** Others work together to improve trade among the members.

Like the United Nations, these organizations are not a form of government. They do not make laws or have armies. Rather, they offer governments a way to work together. One nation can belong to many different groups.

NATO members in 1999 included Belgium, Canada, the Czech Republic, Denmark, France, Germany, Greece, Hungary, Iceland, Italy, Luxembourg, the Netherlands, Norway, Poland, Portugal, Spain, Turkey, the United Kingdom, and the United States.

Like the United Nations, NATO has the ability to send peacekeeping forces from member nations to places where there is conflict.

As these countries work together, their economic strength grows.

One of the oldest organizations is the North Atlantic Treaty Organization (NATO). NATO was formed after **World War II.** Twelve countries, including the United States, promised to come to one another's aid in case of another war or conflict. Over time, the organization has changed. Nineteen NATO countries now work together to try and bring about peace without having to use force.

ASEAN members in 1999 included Brunei, Indonesia, Laos, Malaysia, Myanmar (Burma), the Philippines, Singapore, Thailand, and Vietnam.

The Association of Southeast Asian Nations (ASEAN) was formed in 1967 to help the economies of countries in Southeast Asia grow. These countries realized that when their governments worked together, they could create more wealth than if each country worked alone.

The European Union

If you take a five-hour train trip in the United States, you may go through one or more states. But you will still be in the same country, able to spend the same money. Almost everyone you meet will speak the same language.

In Europe, on the other hand, a five-hour train trip will take you through at least two, maybe even three, different countries. Each country has its own money and language.

Some European nations began to work together about fifty years ago to rebuild their countries after **World War II.** They discovered that if they worked with their neighbor nations, they would be able to rebuild faster, and the less likely it was that they would go to war against one another again.

In 1999, EU members included Austria, Belgium, Denmark, Finland, France, Germany, Greece, Ireland, Italy, Luxembourg, the Netherlands, Portugal, Spain, Sweden, and the United Kingdom. The number is likely to increase in coming years.

*In some EU countries, people can use **currency** called the euro. Stores post prices both in euros and in the local currency.*

The European Union began as an economic organization, but today it deals with issues that range from law enforcement to politics.

They founded a simple organization called the European **Economic Union** (known as the Common Market) to break down barriers that made it difficult to trade with so many different countries. Today, this simple idea has turned into the European Union, or EU, which now has fifteen member nations and a **legislature**—the European **Parliament.** Countries that join the European Union do not have to give up their constitutions or change their governments. They do not have give up their own languages.

The main purpose of the EU is to bring the people in the separate countries of Europe closer together. It is now easier for people to travel from one country to another and for each country to buy from or sell to each other. The EU has also developed a currency called the Euro that will replace the many different currencies used by most member countries.

Glossary

absolute ruler ruler with the power to make all the laws, enforce all the laws, and decide the punishment for breaking the laws; ruler with unlimited power

authority power to enforce laws, command obedience, or judge

authoritarian power is in the hands of one or a few individuals

benefit something provided by a government to its citizens, such as health care, education, housing, or retirement income

capitalism economic system in which individuals may own natural resources, factories, and products, and may keep the money they make from selling them

chief executive top person in the executive branch

chief of state person who is the head of a national government

communist economic system in which natural resources, land, factories, and products are owned by all people in the community, and all citizens share the money that is made from selling them

confederation group of provinces or territories that band together

conflict situation in which groups of people or countries strongly disagree with one another and may possibly fight

constitution written document describing the basic laws or principles by which a government is organized; a description of power and its limits

currency money used in a country

democracy rule by the majority of the people who are governed

document written or printed paper

economic having to do with the the way that a country manages its money and the products it makes and uses

enforce to make people obey

federal referring to a group of states that give up some power to a central government

free-market economy system of trade that permits individuals to make and sell as many items as they like

hereditary passed on by parents or ancestors

income tax money paid to a government based on the amount of money a person earns

interfere to get in the way of

legislature group of people with power to make and change a nation's laws, also called a parliament

military armed forces such as the army, marines, or air force

monarch ruler such as a king or queen

overthrow to bring down or cause to fall apart, often by use of force

parliament group of people with power to make and change a nation's laws, also called a legislature

political having to do with government

political party group of people who have similar views about government

popular vote election in which ordinary citizens make their choices known

prime minister high government official often appointed by a ruler or chosen by the political party with the most members in the legislature

profit money earned when an item is sold for more than it cost to make

province political unit of a nation or empire; similar to a state

raw material something that can be made into another product after being processed in some way

republic government in which the citizens hold the power and elect individuals to serve as leaders and representatives

socialist relating to the belief that a government should own the means of producing goods so that no one is poor

Soviet Union communist country that included Russia and other nations, and that was divided into separate countries in 1991

trade business of buying and selling goods

totalitarian relating to a government that attempts to control every part of a person's life

welfare providing funds for health care and a minimum standard of living for those who can't afford these things

World War II war involving Great Britain, France, the Soviet Union, and the United States against Germany, Italy, and Japan—as well as the allies of these nations—fought in Europe, Asia, and Africa from 1939 to 1945

More Books to Read

Armbruster, Ann. *The United Nations*. New York: Franklin Watts, 1995.

Bradley, John. *Russia: Building Democracy*. Austin, Tex.: Raintree Steck-Vaughn, 1995.

Mayberry, Jodine. *Leaders Who Changed the Twentieth Century*. Austin, Tex.: Raintree Steck-Vaughn, 1993.

Pietrusza, David. *The End of the Cold War*. San Diego: Lucent Books, 1994.

Index